The Enormous Turnip

Retold and dramatised from an old Russian
story as a reading play
for partners or small groups.

Ellie Hallett

Where are the pictures?
Why there is just one illustration?

In this story, the words create the pictures. While you are reading, pictures of the action will come into your mind. This means that not only are you the reader, you are also the artist!

This story is suitable for school and home. Some 'how to read' ideas are below.

- With a partner or small group, take it in turns to read the rows.

- Don't rush! This helps you to say each word clearly.

- Think of yourselves as actors by adding lots of facial and vocal expression. Small gaps of silence also create dramatic energy. These techniques will bring the story to life.

- If you meet a new word, try to break it down and then say it again. If you have any problems, ask your teacher or a reading buddy.

- Don't be scared of unusual words. They will become your new best friends.
  (New words strengthen your general knowledge and enable you to become vocabulary-rich in your day-to-day life.)

Have fun!

Once upon a time a man found a packet of seeds in an old glass jar.

It had been sitting on a dark and dusty shelf in his tool shed for many years.

He wondered what sort of plant it would be if he planted it in his garden.

He found a spot in his vegetable patch and started to dig.

When the ground was ready, in went the mystery seed.

The man and his wife watered and checked it every morning.

And then one fine day, a little green shoot pushed itself out of the ground.

It stretched up tall and fresh into the bright sunshine.

The man saw it and rushed to tell his wife the exciting news.

'Our mystery seed has sprouted, my dear! Come and have a look!'

'Oh yes! You're right! And if I'm not mistaken, this new arrival in our garden is a turnip.'

After another week the man and his wife noticed something else.

'Our turnip is growing faster than turnips normally grow!'

'We seem to have a champion on our hands, and that's a fact!'

The turnip kept growing faster and bigger and stronger than ever.

The man made sure caterpillars weren't eating the leaves.

The wife pulled out even the smallest of weeds.

Next door's cat checked that there were no mice having turnip snacks.

And the turnip kept growing.

News soon spread all around the town about the huge turnip.

Children arrived after school and on the weekends to ask questions.

'Where did you get the seed?'

'How much compost do you use?'

'Is this an organic turnip?'

'Will you mulch the leaves?'

'At what depth do the roots go down into the sub-strata?'

'Is acid or alkaline soil better?'

And someone always asked about pulling the turnip out of the ground.

'When do you think your turnip will be ready to harvest?'

And the man and his wife replied with a twinkle in their eyes …

'In another week or so.'

The children told their parents about the massive turnip.

It wasn't long before they wanted to have a look for themselves.

The parents asked the man and his wife a lot of questions.

'A turnip that big must need a lot of watering and mulching.'

'How are you ever going to cook a turnip this big?'

'Aren't you worried it'll explode?'

'Can I pat your guard cat please?'

'What are the health benefits of turnips?'

'How many vitamins and minerals does a turnip have?'

'When are you going to pull that turnip out of the ground?'

And the man and his wife replied with a twinkle in their eyes …

'In another week or so.'

A few days later, a bus driver spoke to the man and his wife.

He wanted to bring a bus-load of tourists to visit.

And, of course, the tourists asked more questions than anyone else.

'Why do you like turnips?'

'Where is your souvenir shop?'

'Don't you worry that your turnip will split in half?'

'What is the name of your cat?'

'How do you stop bugs eating it?'

'What about snails and moths and grubs?'

'Do you use a bucket or a hose to water your turnip?'

'What sort of turnip *is* it exactly?'

'How do you stop weeds?'

'Do you also grow enormous onions?'

'Why don't I try and pull it out for you?'

'What if it's starting to rot in the ground, buddy?'

'My grandpa grew a bigger one than that, but it turned out to be a carrot!'

'And when did you say you are going to pull it out?'

The man and his wife replied with a twinkle in their eyes …

'In another week or so.'

Now, it so happened that one sunny day when the birds were singing, the man spoke to his wife.

'I think the time has come at last to harvest our enormous turnip.'

'Funny you should say that, dear husband. I have just found a recipe called *Tasty Turnip Tart*.'

'It sounds delicious! It is absolutely and definitely time to dig out our turnip!'

And so a plan was put into action.

'Here's your big straw hat!'

'Will we need gardening gloves?'

'How about the big fork?'

'We might even need a spade.'

'I'll put on my heavy boots.'

'I'll bring the wheelbarrow.'

'I'm really looking forward to a slice of *Tasty Turnip Tart*!'

'Well – here we go, dear husband!'

'Yes, dear wife. Our adventure is about to start!'

'I don't think this'll take long.'

'Should be out in ten minutes.'
'First I'll loosen the soil.' *(pause)*
'You seem to be digging a long way down!'
'Yes! But I think it's on its way! I definitely heard something.'
'How exciting! This turnip is going to be world famous!'
'Sadly No. False alarm. Can't seem to budge it one little bit!'
'Perhaps a more hands-on approach, dear husband?'

'I agree. I'll grip the leaves and pull with all my might.'

But the harder the man pulled, the deeper the turnip seemed to go.

'I need your help, dear wife!'

'One, two, three, *pull!*'

But the enormous turnip didn't want to be pulled. It stayed stuck.

The children arrived to find out what was happening.

'Want a hand with that turnip?'

'Yes, please. Just go to the end of the line.'

The husband held onto the turnip.

The wife held onto the husband.

The children held onto the wife.

'One, two, three, *pull!*'

But - that enormous turnip stayed exactly where it was.

The parents arrived to see what was happening.

'Want a hand with that turnip?'

'Yes, please! Just go to the end of the line.'

The husband held onto the turnip.

The wife held onto the husband.

The children held onto the wife.

The parents held onto the children.

'One, two, three, *pull!*'

But the turnip still stayed put.

The bus driver arrived with yet another load of tourists.

These tourists were a noisier lot.

They yelled and pushed each other trying to be first out of the bus.

And then they each ran as fast as they could to have the best view of the turnip.

Cameras were put on tripods.

The sun's direction was checked.

Sips of water were taken.

Hats were taken off and put on.

Voices became louder and faster.

The bus driver decided that he had had enough.

He was sick of these pushy passengers. He called out in his loudest voice ...

'**Quiet**! I can't hear myself think!'

Everyone stopped talking and stared, their mouths open.

In a quiet voice, the bus driver spoke to the man and his wife.

'Want a hand with that turnip?'

'Yes, please.'

The husband held onto the turnip.

The wife held onto the husband.

The children held onto the wife.

The parents held onto the children.

The bus driver held onto the parents.

'One, two, three, *pull!*'

'I heard something.'

'Hooray! It's on its way!'

'Let's give it another try!'
'Ready, set, *pull!*'
'Oh no! It's deeper than ever.'
They crossed their eyes as they pulled.
They dug their heels into the ground.
They took deep breaths in and out.
'Woof! Woof!'
It was Roxy, the bus driver's dog.
Her tail was wagging faster than it had ever wagged before.

Into the garden she bounded, looking for her owner.

Roxy wanted to join in the fun.

She liked this game called *Pull,* and she barked excitedly.

Once again the husband gripped the turnip leaves as hard as he could.

The wife held onto the husband.

The children held onto the wife.

The parents held onto the children.

The bus driver held onto the parents.

And Roxy pulled on the bus driver's coat tail.

'One, two, three, *pull!*'
'Here it comes!'
'She's out at last!
'Unbelievable.'
'What a whopper!'
The husband fell over.
The wife fell over.
The children fell over.
The parents fell over.
And the bus driver fell over.
The tourists took lots of photos.
Roxy did a double somersault.

Next door's cat ran up a tree.

And then everyone began to laugh more loudly than they had ever laughed before.

Roxy barked so much that she started to squeak.

The tourists suddenly yelled out.

They had fallen into the enormous hole left by the enormous turnip.

They were tangled in tripods and as messy as mud pies.

Each pushed and slid and slipped trying to be first out of the hole.

Roxy rolled on the grass with happiness.

Up in the tree, the cat yawned and decided to have a wash.

When everyone was at last back to normal, the man and his wife made an important announcement.

'You are invited to lunch next Saturday for *Tasty Turnip Tart*.'

And that is exactly what happened.

And as you might have guessed, that *Tasty Turnip Tart* was the best that anyone had ever tasted.